Aus der Dunkelheit ins Licht

story:
Jennifer Degenhardt

translator:
Julie Young

editor:
Brigitte Kahn

illustrator:
Juliette Chattaway

All rights reserved. No part of this publication may be reproduced, stored in a retrieval system, or transmitted in any form or by any means - electronic, mechanical, photocopying, recording or otherwise – without prior written permission of the authors, except for brief passages quoted by a reviewer in a newspaper, magazine or blog. To perform any of the above is an infringement of copyright law.

Copyright © 2023 Jennifer Degenhardt (Puentes)
All rights reserved.
ISBN: 978-1-956594-45-4

This story is for all who experience challenges with their mental health.
May you find your ray of sunshine.

AUTHOR'S NOTE

Hello!

Thank you for taking the time to read this message before you start reading. It's important that you know what you might find in the pages so you can make a reasonable choice whether or not to dive in.

This story deals with inner turmoil and associated dark thoughts, up to and including those of self-harm. I did not write this story to be triggering to anyone, but rather - as always - to provide an opportunity for discussion. It is my hope that by sharing a story that is based on feelings that I have had personally, that I can help with the discussion about self-harm, suicidal thoughts and the spiral that the human mind can get itself into. Yes, you read that right: I have struggled with depression and delicate mental health for many years, which ultimately led to some really negative thinking. While it is not a time in my life that I wish to revisit, I am grateful for the experience, as it has changed the way I view everything in life.

The first and best thing I did was to ask for help. And I didn't just ask one person, I asked many. Family and friends were there for me, as I know that family and friends would be for anyone, if the person in need simply asks for help.

This story is meant to serve as a jumping-off point to talk about mental health and to provide one look into the anxiety that some experience. Furthermore, since each person's journey is different, the novel ends with possibility. In no way does the ending mean to suggest that struggles such as these can be easily taken care of with an ice cream, a flower or even a puppy. Still, I wanted to end with some hope for better days - like the ones I am so fortunate enough to experience now.

The subject matter is difficult. Please read with care.

-Jen Degenhardt
September 2023

You aren't going to feel this way forever, you know.

The mind has thoughts, and those thoughts control your feelings.

It will all be okay in the end. If it's not okay, it's not the end.

Try to think positively. Everything in life – including the bad – is temporary.

I imagine that your path in life will be a little difficult for a while, but it won't be forever. Everything will get better.

Remember: your thoughts control your feelings. And you can change your thoughts.

DANKE

You are reading this story in German thanks to the dynamic duo of Julie Young and Brigitte Kahn. Julie is responsible for the translation, and Brigitte, the editing. As both are German teachers who use these types of novels with their own students, you can be sure that comprehensibility is top of mind. *Danke* to both of you for all your efforts to get this story spiffed up and ready for publication!

Having had this story in mind for a while, I started it on the plane on a return flight from California, I think it was. I had done the preparation, taken the notes and had begun writing furiously. And then somehow, I deleted the file. Like, really deleted it, not just in file purgatory. Ugh.

But I had already hired the artist. Juliet Chattaway was still in elementary school when I asked her to draw a teenager in a hoodie, in a bedroom with one window. I then asked her to alter the drawings a bit at a time (I don't want to give it away!), so they too, could be part of the story. Juliet understood my vision exactly, even when I might not always have been so clear. It is a pleasure and an honor to work with student artists like Juliet. Thank you, Juliet!

I owe the following people a huge debt of gratitude (and if you're reading this, or any of my books, so do you. 😉) If not for these people to whom I reached out for help those few years ago, I may not have had the opportunity to write this story - or any others for that matter. I am grateful to each of you. Thank you.

Sarah Jessup & Robert Allen
Celia Bartholomew & John Bartholomew
Angela Degenhardt
Claire Degrigrio
Tara Allen & José Salazar
Amy Salvin Collins
Wendy Perrotti
Patti Nietsch

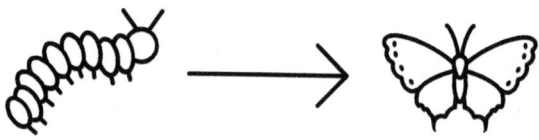

Just when the caterpillar thought the world was over, it became a butterfly...

-proverb

In einem Haus...
oder in einer Wohnung...

Die Tante klopft an die Tür.

Die Tante öffnet die Tür einen Spalt. Alex sitzt in einem dunklen Schlafzimmer auf dem Boden, vor dem Bett.

Die Tante öffnet die Tür ein wenig weiter.

Alex? Geht's dir gut?

Ich ziehe die Jalousien hoch, damit die Sonne hereinkommt.

O.K., Alex. Ich muss für eine Stunde rausgehen. Willst du mit mir kommen? Wir können deine Lieblingssüßigkeiten kaufen, wie wir es früher getan haben...

"O.K. Bist du sicher, dass es dir gut geht? Ich will dich nicht alleine lassen."

O.K. Brauchst du etwas?

Wenn du etwas brauchst, schick mir eine SMS.

Alex, du wirst dich nicht für immer so fühlen, weißt du.

Es wird besser. Du wirst sehen. Ich bin in einer Stunde wieder da. Ruh dich aus.

Alex nimmt die Flasche mit den Pillen. Alex schluchzt. Xier hat große Schmerzen. Xier hat keine Kraft mehr...

Alex nimmt die Pillen aus der Flasche, als xier bewusstlos wird.

Es vergeht viel Zeit.

Die Tante kommt nach Hause. Sie hat eine Schachtel.

Sie bekommt keine Antwort. Man hört nur Hündchen-Geräusche.

Die Tante geht in das Schlafzimmer von Alex. Alex ist auf dem Boden. Die Pillen-Flasche steht auch auf dem Boden.

Die Tante stellt die Schachtel mit dem Hündchen auf den Boden und läuft zu Alex.

Alex öffnet die Augen ein wenig.

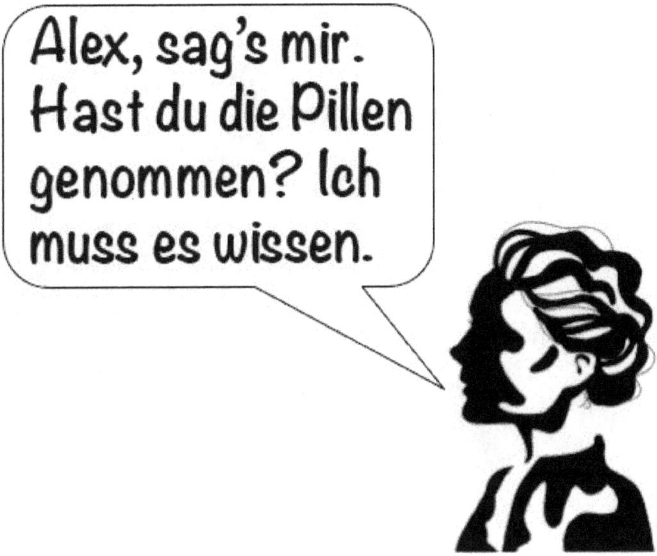
Alex, sag's mir. Hast du die Pillen genommen? Ich muss es wissen.

> Oh, Alex. Mach dir keine Sorgen. Alles wird wieder gut. Du wirst dich nicht für immer so fühlen.

> Deine Eltern haben ihre eigenen Entscheidungen getroffen. Sie sind Erwachsene. Du bist noch ein Kind. Das ist nicht deine Schuld.

In diesem Moment beginnt das Hündchen wieder zu bellen.

Als ich jung war, hatte ich einen Hund namens Sunshine.

Die Tante bringt die Schachtel und öffnet sie. Das Hündchen springt aus der Schachtel und geht direkt zu Alex.

Wie willst du dein Hündchen nennen?

"Denk an dieses Sprichwort: "Ende gut, alles gut." Wenn es nicht gut ist, ist es nicht das Ende."

Von einem Freund, einem sehr weisen Freund.

Alex, dein Weg wird eine Zeit lang etwas schwierig sein, aber das wird nicht für immer so bleiben.

"Und schau mal, es ist sonnig draußen. Sollen wir mit Athena nach draußen gehen, damit sie ihre neue Nachbarschaft kennenlernen kann?"

Hey there!
If you need help, or a friend needs help, tell someone. Find a trusted adult who can help, too. And, check out the resources below.
☮❤☺

Suicide and Crisis Lifeline
988 - via phone or text

The Crisis Text Line
Text TALK to 741741

The American Foundation for Suicide Prevention
https://afsp.org/get-help

Outside of the USA
Find a Helpline
https://findahelpline.com/i/iasp

GLOSSAR

A
aber - but
ach - ach
alle - all
alleine - alone
alles - everything
als - as
altes - old
an - on
Ängste - fears, anxieties
(dir etwas) antun - to harm (yourself)
Antwort - answer
armer - poor
attackieren - to attack
auch - also
auf - on
(hör) auf - stop
aufhören - to stop
Augen - eyes
aus - out

B
begann - began
beginnt - begins
bei - at
beim - at the
bekommen - to get
bekommt - gets
bellen - to bark
berühmt - famous
besser(e) - better
bestohlen - stolen from
Bett - bed
bewusstlos - unconscious
bezahlen - to pay
bin - I am
bis - until
bisschen - a little
bist - you are
bitte - please
bleiben - to stay
Boden - floor
brauche - I need
brauchst - you need
bringt - brings
Bruder - brother

D
dachte - thought
damit - so that
danke - thank you
dann - then

darüber - about that
darf - may
das - the
dass - that
dein(e)(em)(en)(er)(es) - your
dem - the
den - the
denk - think
denken - to think
Depression(en) - depression(s)
der - the
des - of the
dich - you
die - the
diese(m)(n)(r)(s) - this
Dinge - things
dir - you
direkt - direct
draußen - outside
du - you
Dunkelheit - darkness
dunklen - dark

E
eigen(en)(es) - own
ein(e)(em)(en)(er)(es) - a
Eltern - parents
Ende - end
endgültigen - final
Entscheidungen - decisions
er - he
ertragen - to endure
Erwachsene - adults
Erwachsener - adult
es - it
etwas - something

F
(nichts) Falsches - (nothing) wrong
Familie - family
Feigling - coward
finanzielle - financial
finanzieren - to finance
Flasche - bottle
früher - in former times
fühlen - to feel
Freund - friend
für - for

G
ganze - whole, entire
Gedanken - thoughts
Gefängnis - prison
Gefühle - feelings
gegangen - gone
geh - go
gehen - to go
geholfen - helped
geht - s/he goes
Geist - mind, spirit
Geld - money
gelandet - landed
gelernt - learned
gemacht - made, did
genommen - taken
Geräusche - noises
gestohlen - stolen
getan - done
getroffen - met
getrunken - drank
Gewalt - violence
gewinnen - to win
gewonnen - won
gib - give
gibst - you give
gibst (zu) - you admit
glücklich - happy
Göttin - goddess
große - big
gut(e)(es) - good

H
habe - I have
haben - to have
hast - you have
hat - s/he has
hatte - I, s/he had
hatten - they had
hätte - would have
hättest - you would have
Haus - house
(nach) Hause - (to) home
helfe - I help
helfen - to help
hereinkommt - s/he comes in
hier - here
hilf - help
hilft - s/he helps
hoch(ziehen) - to lift up
hört - hears
Hund - dog
Hündchen - puppy
Hündchen Geräusche - puppy noises

I
ich - I
Idee - idea
ihn - him
ihre - her, their
im - in the
immer - always
in - in
innere - internal
ins - in the
ist - is

J
ja - yes
Jalousien - blinds
jedem - every
jedes - every
jetzt - now
jung - young

K
kam - came
kann - can
kannst - you can
kaufen - to buy
kein(e) - not any
kennenlernen - to get to know
Kind - child
klar - clear
kleines - small
klopft - knocks
kommen - to come
kommt - comes
kompliziert - complicated
können - we could
konnte - could
könnte - could
könntest - you could
Kontrolle - control
kontrollieren - to control
Körper - body
kosten - to cost
Kraft - strength
Krankenhaus - hospital
Krimineller - criminal
Kunde(n) - customer(s)

L
lang - long
lass - leave
lassen - to leave
läuft - runs
leben - to live

Leben - life
(Rest deines) Lebens - rest of your life
letzten - last
lieber - prefer
Lieblingssüßigkeiten - favorite candies
lügst - you lie

M
mach - make
machen - to make, do
Mädchen - girl
mag - I, s/he likes
Mal - time
man - one
Medizin - medicine
mehr - more
mein(e)(em)(er)(es) - my
meinst - you mean
mich - me
mir - to me
mit - with
Moment - moment
muss - I, s/he must
musst - you must
musste - I, s/he must
mussten - they had to
Mut - courage
(des) Mutes - of courage
Mutter - mother

N
na(gut) - alright
nach - to
Nachbarschaft - neighborhood
nachdenken - to think about
nachdenkst - you think about
nächste - next
nachzudenken - in order to think about
Name - name
namens - called
natürlich - of course
nehmen - to take
nein - no
nennen - to name
nett - nice
neue - new
nicht - not
nichts - nothing
nimm - take

nimmst - you take
nimmt - takes
noch - still
normales - normal
nur - only

O
ob - if
oder - or
öffnet - opens
oh - oh
okay - okay

P
Papa - dad
passieren - to happen
(ist)passiert - happened
perfekt - perfect
Perfektion - perfection
Pillen - pills
Plan - plan
Polizei - police
positiv - positive
Preis - price
Problem(e) - problem(s)
problemloses - problem-free
Programm - program
psychologischen - psychological

R
rausgehen - to go out
red - talk
rede - I talk
reden - to talk
reinkommen - to come in
Rest - rest
ruh (dich aus) - rest
Ruhe - peace

S
sag - say
sagen - to say
sagt - says
schön - nice
Schachtel - box
schau - look
schick - send
Schlafzimmer - bedroom
schlecht(e)(en) - bad
Schlimmes - something bad
schluchzt - sobs
Schmerzen - pain
Schuld - guilt

schuldig - guilty
schwierig(en) - difficult
sehen - to see
sehr - very
sein - to be
sein(e)(em)(en) - his
seit - since
Selbstmedikation - self-medication
sicher - sure
sie - she, they
siehst - you see
sind - they are
Situation - situation
sitzt - sits
SMS - text (on cellphone)
so - so
soll - should
sollen - they should
solltest - you should
Sonne - sun
sonnig - sunny
Sorgen - worries, cares
Spalt - gap
Sport - sport
Sprichwort - a saying
springt - jumps
Stärke - strengths
steht - stands
stellt - puts
Stimme - voice
(es) stimmt - it's true
Stipendium - scholarship
Stunde - hour
super - super

T
Tante - aunt
teilgenommen - took part
teilnehmen - to take part
Test - test
teure(n) - expensive
trainieren - to train
trainiert - trains
Training - training
trank - drank
traurig - sad
traut - trusts
trinken - to drink
trinkt - drinks
tun (weh) - hurt
tut (weh) - hurts

U
über - about
Überraschung - surprise
um (....zu) - in order to
um - about
und - and
Universität - university
uns - us
Unterstüzung - support

V
Vater - father
verbessern - to improve
Verbrechen - crime
verdrängen - suppress
vergeht - passes
vergessen - forgotten
Verhaftung - arrest
verletzen - to injure
verletzt - injured
Verletzung - injury
Verständnis - understanding
verstehe - I understand
versuche - I try
viel - a lot
vielleicht - perhaps
von - from
vor - in front of
vorbei - over
vorher - previously

W
wach - awake
war - was
wäre - would be
warst - you were
warum - why
was - what
Weg - path
weg - away
weglaufen - to run away
(tut) weh - hurts
wehtun - to hurt
weiß - I know
weißt - you know
weil - because
weinen - to cry
weinst - you cry
weint - cries
weisen - wise
weiter - further
weiterkommen - to progress, to get ahead

weitermachen - to continue
wen - whom
wenig - a little
(mehr oder) **weniger** - more or less
wenn - when, if
werde - I will
werden - they will
(gut) werden - become good
wertlos - worthless
Wettbewerb - competition
wie - like, how
wie (viel) - how much
wieder - again
will - I, s/he wants
willst - you want
wir - we
wird - s/he will
wirklich - really
wirst - you will
wissen - to know
woher - from where
Wohnung - apartment
wollte - I, s/he wanted
wolltest - you wanted
würde - would
würdest - you would
wusste - I, s/he knew
wusstest - you knew

X
xier - they (non binary pronoun)

Z
Zeit - time
Zerstörung - destruction
ziehe (hoch) - I lift up
zu - to
zugesehen - watched
Zukunft - future
zum - to the
zur - to the
zurückgeben - to give back

ABOUT THE AUTHOR

Jennifer Degenhardt taught high school Spanish for over 20 years and now teaches at the college level. At the time she realized her own high school students, many of whom had learning challenges, acquired language best through stories, so she began to write ones that she thought would appeal to them. She has been writing ever since.

Other titles by Jen Degenhardt:

La chica nueva \ *La Nouvelle Fille* \ The New Girl \ *Das Neue Mädchen* \ *La nuova ragazza*
La chica nueva (the ancillary/workbook volume, Kindle book, audiobook)
Salida 8 / Sortie no. 8
Chuchotenango \ *La terre des chiens errants* \ *La vita dei cani*

Pesas | Poids et haltères | <u>Weights and Dumbbells</u> | Pesi
Luis, un soñador
El jersey | <u>The Jersey</u> | Le Maillot
La mochila | <u>The Backpack</u> | Le sac à dos
Moviendo montañas | Déplacer les montagnes | <u>Moving Mountains</u> | Spostando montagne
La vida es complicada | La vie est compliquée | <u>Life is Complicated</u>
La vida es complicada Practice & Questions (workbook)
El Mundial | La Coupe du Monde | <u>The World Cup</u>
Quince | <u>Fifteen</u> | Douze ans
Quince Practice & Questions (workbook)
El viaje difícil | Un voyage difficile | <u>A Difficult Journey</u>
La niñera
¡¿Fútbol...americano?! | Football...américain ?!
Era una chica nueva
Levantando pesas: un cuento en el pasado
Se movieron las montañas
Fue un viaje difícil
¿Qué pasó con el jersey?
Cuando se perdió la mochila
Con (un poco de) ayuda de mis amigos | <u>With (a little) Help from My Friends</u> | Un petit coup de main amical
Con (un po') d'aiuto dai miei amici
La última prueba | <u>The Last Test</u>
Los tres amigos | <u>Three Friends</u> | Drei Freunde | Les trois amis

La evolución musical
María María: un cuento de un huracán | <u>María María: A Story of a Storm</u> | *Maria Maria: un histoire d'un orage*
Debido a la tormenta | <u>Because of the Storm</u>
La lucha de la vida | <u>The Fight of His Life</u>
Secretos | *Secrets* | <u>Secrets Undisclosed</u>
Como vuela la pelota
Cambios | *Changements* | <u>Changes</u>
De la oscuridad a la luz | <u>From Darkness into Light</u> | *De la obscurité à la lumière* | Dal buio alla luce | Aus der Dunkelheit ins Licht
El pueblo | <u>The Town</u> | Le village

@JenniferDegenh1

@jendegenhardt9

@PuentesLanguage &
World LanguageTeaching Stories (group)

Visit www.puenteslanguage.com to sign up to receive information on new releases and other events.

Check out all titles as ebooks with audio on www.digilangua.co.

ABOUT THE ILLUSTRATOR

Juliet Chattaway is a sixth-grade student at New Canaan Country School. She has loved art all her life and draws after school every day. In addition to drawing, Juliet spends her free time reading and writing short stories. One day, she hopes to publish her own Webtoon or book. Juliet lives in Darien, CT with her mother, father and younger brother, Nicholas.

www.ingramcontent.com/pod-product-compliance
Lightning Source LLC
Chambersburg PA
CBHW071223090426
42736CB00014B/2949